Congressional
Research Service
Informing the legislative debate since 1914

U.S. Foreign-Trade Zones: Background and Issues for Congress

Mary Jane Bolle
Specialist in International Trade and Finance

Brock R. Williams
Analyst in International Trade and Finance

November 12, 2013

Congressional Research Service

7-5700

www.crs.gov

R42686

Summary

U.S. foreign-trade zones (FTZs) are geographic areas declared to be outside the normal customs territory of the United States. This means that, for foreign merchandise entering FTZs and re-exported as different products, customs procedures are streamlined and tariffs do not apply. For products intended for U.S. consumption, full customs procedures are applied and duties are payable when they exit the FTZ.

In 1934, in the midst of the Great Depression, Congress passed the U.S. Foreign-Trade Zones Act. It was designed to expedite and encourage international trade while promoting domestic activity and investment. The U.S. FTZ program offers a variety of customs benefits to businesses which combine foreign and domestic merchandise in FTZs. Similar types of "zones" exist in 135 countries, employing about 66 million workers worldwide. Though some aspects differ, all have streamlined customs procedures and no duties applicable on components and raw materials combined in zones and then exported. Use of the zones can facilitate cooperative international production for a substantial share of the global supply chain.

U.S. FTZs can affect the competitiveness of U.S. companies by allowing savings through (1) duty reduction on "inverted tariff structures" (where tariffs are higher on imported components than on finished products); (2) customs and inventory efficiencies; and (3) duty exemption on goods exported from, or consumed, scrapped, or destroyed in, a zone. Though difficult to achieve, other possible alternatives, such as broad-based tariff reductions through multilateral negotiations, and overall customs reform might provide some of the same competitive advantages as zone use in a more efficient manner, while also ensuring that all importers have equal access.

Zone activity represents a significant share of U.S. trade. In 2012, over 13% of foreign goods entered the United States through FTZs or bonded warehouses—72% of them as crude oil. Most shipments arriving through FTZs were consumed in the United States; the rest were exported. Crude oil byproducts such as gasoline, diesel, jet fuel, kerosene, and petrochemicals dominate FTZ output. Other key products include autos, consumer electronics, and machinery. U.S. zone activity occurs primarily in FTZ manufacturing operations.

Administration of the U.S. FTZ system is overseen by the Secretaries of Commerce and the Treasury, who constitute the U.S. FTZ Board. The Board is responsible for the establishment of zones, the authorization of specific production activity, and the general oversight of zones. It also appoints an Executive Secretary, who oversees the Board's staff. Homeland Security's Customs and Border Protection (CBP) directly oversees FTZs. It activates the zones and secures and controls dutiable merchandise moving into and out of them. CBP oversight also includes both protection of U.S. tariff revenue and protection from illegal activity through screening, targeting, and inspections.

In 2012, the U.S. FTZ Board issued new regulations. They focused primarily on streamlining the application procedures and shortening, generally from a year to four months, the time for FTZ approval for manufacturing.

Congressional Interest

Congress has demonstrated a continuing interest in U.S. Foreign Trade Zones (FTZs), as they (1) may help to maintain U.S. employment opportunities and the competitiveness of U.S. producers;

(2) encompass a portion of U.S. trade; and (3) affect U.S. tariff revenue. U.S. FTZs account for less than one-half of 1% of all world zone workers and a small share of the U.S. workforce. However, most of this employment is in manufacturing, which has lost a significant share of its workers over the past several decades. Today, every state has at least one FTZ, and many have numerous manufacturing operations.

Current issues for Congress relating to the U.S. FTZ program may include (1) whether U.S. FTZs encourage a misallocation of U.S. resources; (2) data availability issues; (3) security concerns; and (4) the U.S. employment and global competitiveness impact of FTZs. Broader considerations relating to the world zone network include (5) the effectiveness of trade zones worldwide as a tool for economic development; and (6) trade zones worldwide and worker rights.

Contents

Figures

Tables

Appendixes

Contacts

Introduction

Members of Congress have demonstrated their interest in the U.S. Foreign-Trade Zone (FTZ) system through hearings and legislation over the past seven decades. The program may enhance the competitiveness of U.S. businesses, support employment opportunities, and impact U.S. tariff revenues. Balancing these potential gains, others argue that the program may also be trade distorting, and may play a role in misallocating resources in the economy as a whole.

This report provides a general perspective on the U.S. FTZ system. It is divided into three parts. As background, the first section discusses free trade zones worldwide. The second section focuses on the U.S. FTZ program—its history, administrative mechanism, structure, growth and industry concentration, and benefits and costs. The third section focuses on current issues for Congress relating to the U.S. FTZ program.

Background on Free Trade Zones

Free Trade Zones Around the World

Foreign-trade zones (FTZs)[1] are the U.S. version of *free trade zones* scattered around the world. Zones elsewhere are called by many different names (See **Text Box 1**.)

Many Names: Variations on a Theme (Text Box 1)
Free trade zones around the world are called by a number of different names, depending on the country in which they are located and the particular type of zone. In the United States, they are referred to as *foreign-trade zones*. Those in developing countries producing specifically for export are typically called *export processing zones*. They are also called *special economic zones* in China, *industrial free zones* or *export free zones* in Ireland, *Qualifying Industrial Zones* (QIZs) in Jordan and Egypt, *free zones* in the United Arab Emirates, and *duty free export processing zones* in the Republic of Korea.

Free trade zones are a specific type of restricted access (e.g., fenced-in) industrial park housing concentrations of production facilities and related infrastructure. They are typically located at or near sea, air, or land ports.

Free trade zones have become a substantial part of the structure underpinning the global supply chain. Together, these roughly 3,500 zones in 135 countries, including the United States[2] (see **Figure 1**), form a web that frees producers from most customs procedures and offer duty savings, thus facilitating intricate international co-production operations.

---

[1] For general information on foreign-trade zones see the Department of Commerce, International Trade Administration's Frequently Asked Questions section of the Foreign-Trade Zones Board website at http://ia.ita.doc.gov/ftzpage/info/ftzstart.html.

[2] International Labor Organization (ILO), ILO *Database on Export Processing Zones (Revised)*, by Jean-Pierre Singa Boyenge, Working Paper, April 2007, Geneva; database developed by the World Bank in conjunction with the World Economic Processing Zones Association (WEPZA), and included in the Multi-donor Investment Climate Advisory Service of the World Bank Group, *Special Economic Zones: Performance, Lessons Learned, and Implications for Zone Development*, 2008.

Although the rules vary by country, the general mechanism that makes them function together in international co-production is that while zones are located *inside* the geographic boundaries of countries, they are generally declared to be *outside* of these countries for customs purposes. Thus, components may be shipped into a zone—and sometimes shifted around the world from zone to zone on their way to becoming a finished product—without concern for tariffs, quotas, and detailed customs procedures, until they finally exit the zone system. Only then are tariffs payable, quotas honored, and full customs procedures applicable. (See **Text Box 2** for examples of the use of one or more zones in a production chain.)

Some analysts argue that free trade zones, in bypassing many of the complexities of individual country tariff assessments and customs procedures, have been one factor facilitating global supply chains. Today, free trade zones employ at least 66 million workers worldwide, including 370,000 in the United States. Most zones are located in developing countries, and most, but not all, of their workers are in manufacturing. Although these workers represent a substantial percentage of the worldwide manufacturing population, their exact share is difficult to estimate.[3] **Figure 1** shows worldwide employment apportionment across zones by geographic region in 2006, the most recent data available. It shows that China accounted for more than 60% (40 million) of world employment in zones; the rest of Asia accounted for 22% (15 million); Mexico and Central America for 8% (5.3 million); and the Middle East/North Africa for 3% (1.7 million); while the United States accounted for 0.5% (320,000).[4]

> **Examples of How the World Zone Network Functions**
> **(Text Box 2)**
>
> 1) Suppose buttons from Indonesia and fabric from India are sent to a trade zone in the Philippines for assembly into a shirt which is then exported to the United States. No tariffs are payable in the Philippines, and all customs procedures are streamlined until the completed shirt enters the United States for consumption.
>
> If, when shipped to the United States, the shirt first enters a U.S. FTZ, taxes and tariffs are only payable if the shirt is eventually imported for consumption—that is, when it exits the FTZ into the customs territory of the United States. It might enter an FTZ for purposes of cost savings, for example, if more work is required (e.g., laundry labels); if some of the shirts were damaged in shipment and will be discarded; or if a company wants to store them for later use (e.g., Christmas sales) and postpone tariff payment.
>
> 2) Similarly, for the production of gasoline, imported crude oil is entered into a refinery which has applied for and received status as an FTZ subzone (i.e., a site approved for a specific company or use). The tariff structure on refined oil products varies, such that some, like gasoline, have much higher tariffs than crude oil, while others, including certain petrochemicals, have a zero tariff, and hence an *inverted tariff structure*. If the refined products exit the zone and are imported into U.S. customs territory, the company can *choose* to pay tariffs on the crude oil that initially entered the zone, or the tariffs (if any) on the refined goods. In addition, chemicals distilled from the crude may stay in the zone or be transferred to a chemical manufacturing facility which is in a nearby subzone for further refining. In the refinery process, as in other production processes in FTZs, tariffs are not payable on any waste products.
>
> **Source:** Examples were constructed by CRS to illustrate possible scenarios.

---

[3] The ILO estimated a number of years ago that there are about 160 million manufacturing workers worldwide. Source: G Betcherman, *An Overview of Labor Markets World-Wide*, 2001. Another difficulty in estimating total world manufacturing employment is that data reports from many countries lag the current year by as much as 10 years.

[4] This number represents about 3% of all U.S. manufacturing employment for 2006, as well as for 2012.

Figure 1. World Geographic Distribution of Employment in Free Trade Zones, 2006

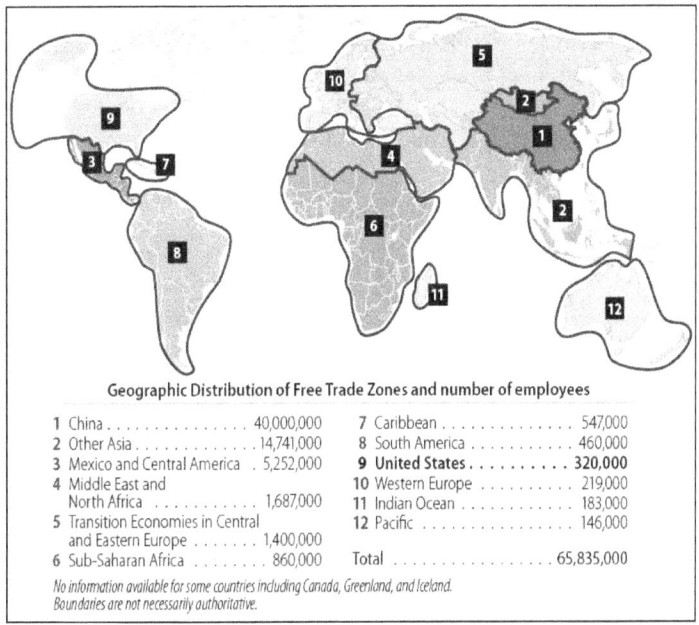

Geographic Distribution of Free Trade Zones and number of employees

1	China	40,000,000	7 Caribbean	547,000
2	Other Asia	14,741,000	8 South America	460,000
3	Mexico and Central America	5,252,000	**9 United States**	**320,000**
4	Middle East and North Africa	1,687,000	10 Western Europe	219,000
5	Transition Economies in Central and Eastern Europe	1,400,000	11 Indian Ocean	183,000
6	Sub-Saharan Africa	860,000	12 Pacific	146,000
			Total	65,835,000

No information available for some countries including Canada, Greenland, and Iceland. Boundaries are not necessarily authoritative.

Source: ILO Database on Export Processing Zones (Revised), by Jean-Pierre Singa Boyenge, Working Paper 251, 2007. The database lists no zones for Canada, although some FTZ-like programs exist. See Virtuosity Consulting, *Canada/US Comparison of Foreign Trade Zone (FTZ) Related Programs and Policies*, March 31, 2009.

Similarities and Differences Among Free Trade Zones Worldwide

Free trade zones around the world are similar in the way they function to facilitate trade. They differ, however, in size, economic development purposes, physical characteristics, government incentives, and the final dispensation of their products. They may represent large shares of the country's manufacturing employment and occupy huge geographic areas, as with special economic zones in China; or they may be small enclaves housing a few businesses. In developing countries with little infrastructure, they may be self-sufficient city-like industrial complexes with housing, dining, and banking, as well as production and/or transport. In developed countries, on the other hand, with extensive infrastructure and modern facilities, they are more narrowly limited to production and/or transport. In the United States, instead of being tied to a specific physical location near port facilities, FTZ designation can quickly and simply be brought to a company, wherever it may be located. All zones typically include streamlined customs procedures and exemption or deferral of tariffs and quotas on stored inventory. Those in developing countries are more likely to have additional incentives such as subsidies, more flexible labor market regulations, and additional tax exemptions.[5] While developing countries typically produce for export, as countries develop, they are increasingly likely to consume ("import") substantial shares of products made in their free trade zones.

---

[5] Subsidies may conflict with some World Trade Organization (WTO) rules, and more flexible labor market regulations may conflict with "best practices" as outlined by the International Labor Organization and the OECD. See, for example, OECD. *Export Processing Zones: Past and Future Role in Trade and Development*, by Michael Engman, Osamu Onodera, and Enrico Pinali, Trade Policy Working Paper No. 53, 2007, p. 8.

Elements common to many free trade zones can be seen in **Figure 2**, below. They include container ships, which can often hold 1,000 to 1,500 containers each, and their automated loading operations; liquid storage tanks (for oil or chemicals, for example); and facilities for transferring individual containers to trucks or to railroad cars.

Figure 2. Elements of Modern Trade Zones

Container Ship Being Loaded

Ship Arriving at Terminal

Liquid Bulk Terminals

Trucks Loaded with Containers

Source: Stock photos from the "LA the Port of Los Angeles" newsroom at http://www.portoflosangeles.org/newsroom.

Growth of Free Trade Zones Worldwide

The growth of zone use over time has resulted from a combination of factors including an initial conceptual design that has stood the test of time; an international mechanism for teaching governments how to establish zones that would attract foreign investors; and major advancements in technology that have supported the globalization of production. **Figure 3** shows the rate at which these factors combined to explode zone use in the past 20 years.

Modern day zone growth began with an "experiment" in 1959, for reuse of the Shannon, Ireland, airport.[6] Designed as a job creation program, it proved so successful that an entrepreneur from the

---

[6] Free trade zones had been used in the Roman Empire and during the Middle Ages, primarily for storage, transshipment, and re-export of goods produced elsewhere. ILO, *Economic and Social Effects of Multinational Enterprises in Export Processing Zones*, 1988, p. 1-3.

Shannon project was asked to help promote the concept through the United Nations. As an advisor to the UN Industrial Development Organization (UNIDO), he reportedly both prepared a manual on zone creation and took part in a number of zone-establishing missions in various countries.[7] The United States government reportedly helped spread the concept of world processing zones when, between 1983 and 1995, five U.S. agencies provided loans and investment support for zone development: the U.S. Agency for International Development (USAID); the Overseas Private Investment Corporation (OPIC); the Export-Import Bank; the Department of State; and the Department of Commerce.[8] Technological developments, including a worldwide telephone/computer/data processing network and advancements in container shipping and other types of transportation encouraged and supported the growth of zones worldwide. Other forces responsible for the proliferation of free trade zones, as identified by the OECD, include the increasing emphasis on both export-oriented and foreign direct investment-oriented growth, the transfer of production of labor intensive industries from developed to developing countries, and the growing international division of labor and incidence of global production networks.[9]

Figure 3. Growth of the World Free Trade Zone System: 1959-2006

	Countries ● =1	Zones	Employees ♀ =100,000
1959	●● 2	1	
1965	●●● 3	2	
1970	●●●●●●●●●● 10	20	50,000
1980	●●●●●●●●●●●●●●●●●●●● 30	NA	NA
1985	●●● 46	175	1,300,000
1990	●● 60	200	2,500,000
1997	NA	845	22,500,000
2006	●●●●●●●●●●●●●●●●●●●●●●●● 135	3,500	66,000,000

Source: United Nations and ILO data. See "Africa, Industrial Policy, and Export Processing Zones: Lessons from Asia," by Howard Stein, Center for Afroamerican and African Studies, University of Michigan, July 2008; and ILO, *Economic and Social Effects of Multinational Enterprises in Export Processing Zones*, 1988, p. 1-2.

Notes: The two countries with zones in 1959 were the United States and Ireland. This ILO zone count excludes early numbers of U.S. zones, which numbered 3 in 1959, 6 in 1965, and 9 in 1970.

---

[7] Ibid., p. 1-3. Later, the World Export Processing Zones Association (WEPZA), originally established by UNIDO, was spun off to become a U.S.-run private, non-profit organization dedicated to assisting the successful development of export processing zones throughout the world. Source: WEPZA website at WEPZA.org.

[8] Walter H. and Dorothy B. Diamond, *Tax-Free Trade Zones of the World*, Unz & Co., 1997, Introduction, p. 33. Between 1977 and 1997, this continually updated three-volume set provided technical information for each country.

[9] OECD, *Export Processing Zones: Past and Future Role in Trade and Development*, by Michael Engman, Osamu Onodera, and Enrico Pinali, OECD Trade Policy Working Paper, No. 53, 2007, p. 8

The U.S. Foreign-Trade Zone Program

History

The U.S. FTZ Program was created by the U.S. Foreign-Trade Zones Act in 1934 (P.L. 73-397, 19 U.S.C. 81[a]-81[u]),[10] in the midst of the Great Depression. It was designed to accelerate U.S. trade in the wake of the restrictive impact of the Smoot-Hawley Tariff Act of 1930, which raised U.S. tariffs on imported goods as high as 53%.[11] It created the FTZ Board, which was given the power to approve applications for zone status. The act, fewer than six pages in length, also entitled each U.S. port of entry to at least one zone, and prescribed physical conditions and standards for each zone, activities permissible in zones, the applicability of all U.S. laws to zones, and requirements for zone operation and recordkeeping.

The FTZ program started slowly. By the time the Shannon experiment was underway 25 years later in 1959, it was still quite small. Gradually, several factors accelerated zone use, including both internal changes to the program itself and external world factors.

Internally, four major things happened. The first and likely the most significant of these factors was changing the program to allow for manufacturing. When the FTZ Act was passed in 1934, it prohibited manufacturing in zones because some feared it would promote imports of cheaper components to be used in the U.S. manufacturing process. At the time, it was argued that U.S. manufacturers of domestic components would be put at risk. That model, however, failed to attract many users. Then, in 1950, Congress amended the FTZ Act to permit manufacturing in zones. Two years later, in 1952, the FTZ Board took that amendment one step further and issued new regulations, which allowed FTZ sites to be designated at a company's facility. It was a way to take zones to the businesses. Additional FTZ growth was encouraged by two U.S. Treasury Department administrative decisions in 1980 and 1982. These clarified that manufacturers need not pay duty on either value-added or brokerage or transportation fees connected with imported goods.[12]

External factors that accelerated FTZ use by U.S and foreign multinational corporations included (1) increased international price competition that led U.S. businesses to seek new ways of saving costs;[13] (2) greater education of businesses in the ways in which they could save money through zone use; and (3) advancements in technology which made cooperative global production possible.

---

[10] Regulations issued by the U.S. Foreign-Trade Zones Board for establishing and maintaining a foreign-trade zone can be found at 15 CFR 400.

[11] Beth V. and Robert M. Yarbrough, *The World Economy: Trade and Finance* (Harcourt Brace, 1991), p. 368.

[12] GAO, *Foreign-Trade Zones Growth Primarily Benefits Users Who Import for Domestic Commerce*, GAO/GGD 84-52, March 2, 1984, p. 12.

[13] U.S. Congress, House, Committee on Government Operations, *Foreign-Trade Zones (FTZ) Program Needs Restructuring*, House Report 101-363, November 16, 1989, p. 11.

The FTZ System Today

Today, the bulk of U.S. FTZ activity occurs in manufacturing operations. The zone can be brought directly to a company's facility, and may be used for manufacturing or warehousing. Across the United States, there were 174 FTZs active during the year, with a total of 276 active manufacturing/production operations. See **Table A-1** for a summary of zone and subzone activity.

All states have at least one zone. Hence, every state has some involvement in the zone system in which foreign and domestic status inputs are combined to make other products. The majority of inputs into zones are of domestic origin (58% or $429 billion) with the remaining inputs (42% or $304 billion) coming from foreign sources. The zone system accounts for 13% of all foreign goods entering the United States and employs roughly 370,000 workers, representing about 3% of U.S. manufacturing workers in 2012—most but not all FTZ employees are in manufacturing. See **Text Box A-1** for details on how FTZs function in terms of moving goods into and out of zones.[14]

Figure 4. U.S. Foreign-Trade Zones, by State
(Approximate Location)

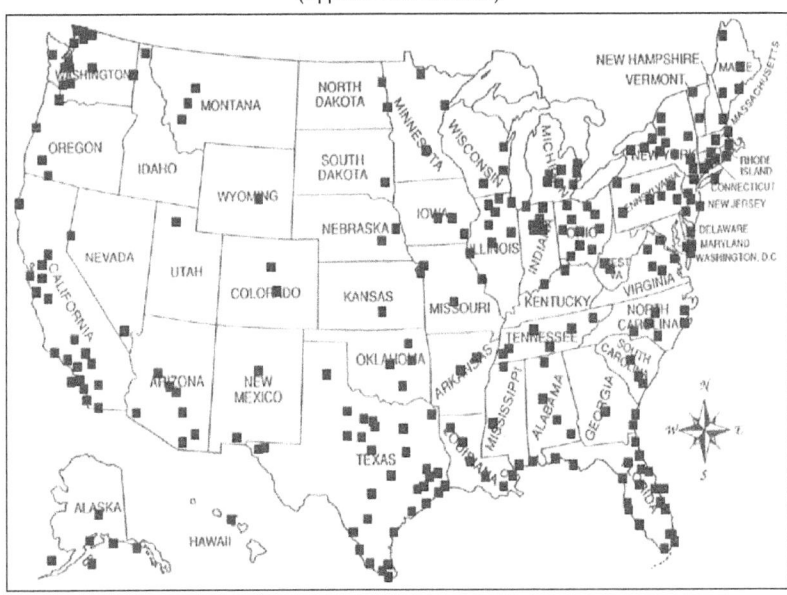

Source: International Trade Administration, Department of Commerce.

Notes: The map is not to scale. The purpose is to show the approximate location and number of Foreign-Trade Zones in each state.

Growth in FTZ Usage and Industry Concentration

Between 1993 and 2012, total foreign and domestic zone inputs (in current dollars) increased more than six-fold (from $104 billion to $732 billion). Much of that increase was due to inflation

---

[14] Except as otherwise indicated, data in these two paragraphs are *from 74th Annual Report of the Foreign-Trade Zones Board to the Congress of the United States*, August 2013.

in the price of crude oil over those 19 years. **Figures 5 and 6,** examine the contributions of foreign and domestic inputs, and figures **7 and 8** examine the contributions of foreign inputs alone, to zone output. From these graphs, several additional observations can be made about zone usage and industry concentration between 1993 and 2012.

- **More U.S. FTZ inputs are produced in the United States than are imported. Figure 5** shows that FTZs are primarily places where smaller shares of foreign inputs (light blue bars) are combined with larger shares of domestic inputs (dark blue bars).

- **Most U.S. FTZ outputs are consumed in the United States.** This is in contrast to *export* processing zones which predominate in developing countries, and from which most outputs are exported. **Figure 6** shows that most of zone output enters the U.S. domestic market (dark blue bars). Only a small share of it is exported (light blue bars).[15]

- **U.S. employment in zones (Figure 5, orange line) has remained relatively steady since 1993.** It rose somewhat during the early 1990s when substantial numbers of labor-intensive auto production companies moved into zones, and has leveled off since then for several reasons, including the following: First, since 1997, FTZs have been used increasingly by petrochemical companies making capital-intensive gasoline, diesel, kerosene, and jet fuels (which benefit from tariff-free storage) and petrochemicals (which benefit from the inverted tariff structure).[16] Second, high levels of inflation in crude oil prices, combined with some increase in productivity, have helped to raise the current value of zone output, while increasing employment slightly.

- **The major foreign input into zones is crude oil.**[17] **Figure 7** shows the current shares of inputs in 2012, by major sector. It shows that crude oil accounts for 72% of all foreign products brought into zones; auto components account for 7%; and other industries, led by consumer electronics and machinery, account for the remaining 21%.[18] The incentive for importing crude oil into zones is to save money on the inverted tariff structure applying to the small share of petrochemicals refined from the crude oil. There are no inverted tariff benefits from the refining of gasoline, diesel, kerosene, and jet fuel, which account for most of the output from crude oil.

- **When foreign oil inputs are deflated[19] to constant dollars, the real (as compared with current) dollar value of foreign inputs into zones shrinks dramatically. Figure 8** compares the value of foreign inputs into zones in current 1993 dollars, in current 2012 dollars, and in 2012 data deflated to constant 1993 dollars. It shows that in 1993, $27 billion in foreign inputs entered FTZs (first bar). In 2012, the value of those inputs into

---

[15] These data exclude value added, for which no figures are available.

[16] Thus, importers can pay the duty-free rate on the final chemicals, instead of the 5.25 or 10.5 cents per barrel that applies to the imported crude oil. However, import tariffs on gasoline and other oil refinements are higher than the tariffs on crude oil, and hence for the share of crude oil used to produce such products, refineries can pay the tariff on the crude rather than the refined products. For auto parts imported from non-free trade agreement countries, the tariffs are typically higher on the imported components than on the completed vehicle.

[17] If the oil component is removed from both FTZ imports and total imports, then remaining non-oil FTZ imports account for just 0.4% of total non-oil U.S. imports.

[18] Oil companies dominate FTZs because petrochemicals (products other than gasoline, diesel, jet fuel, and kerosene) benefit from the inverted tariff structure.

[19] Data for each sector were deflated using the Commerce Department's National Income and Product Accounts Table 4.2.4 Price Indexes for Exports and Imports of Goods and Services by Type of Product.

FTZs was $303 billion. However, once the effect of rising crude oil prices has been netted out, that figure falls to $100 billion in constant 1993 dollars.[20]

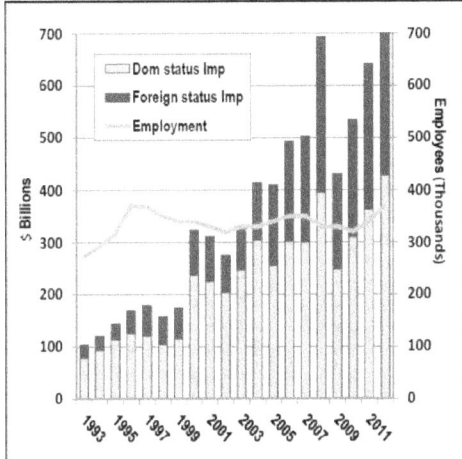

Figure 5. FTZ Input:
Foreign and Domestic Components, and
Employment Levels, 1993-2012

(Current $; right axis for Employment)

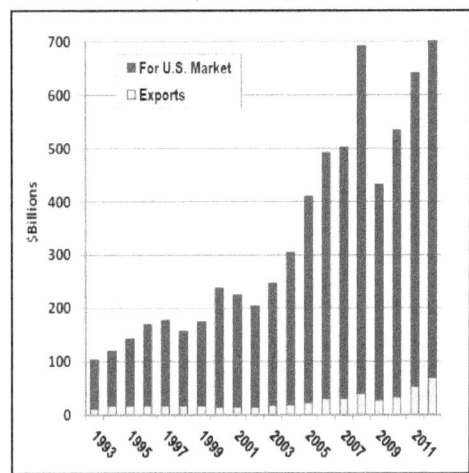

Figure 6. FTZ Output:
Shipment to the U.S. Market, and Exports,
1993-2012

(Current $)

Source: U.S. FTZ Board, Annual Reports to Congress.

Note: Value added and adjustments for "waste" are not included in these figures.

---

[20] For the third bar, each of the three major inputs was deflated using the Commerce Department's National Income and Product Accounts Table 4.2.4 Price Indexes for Exports and Imports of Goods and Services by type of Product. While there are no comparable data for the relative importance of these commodities among "domestic inputs," some level of foreign oil is included in this group along with domestically produced oil. Foreign oil is included because crude oil imports may be entered into zones as "domestic" inputs if they are brought into the United States tariff free under a free trade agreement or other trade preference program.

Figure 7. FTZ Foreign Input Shares, 2012

($303 Billion in Current $)

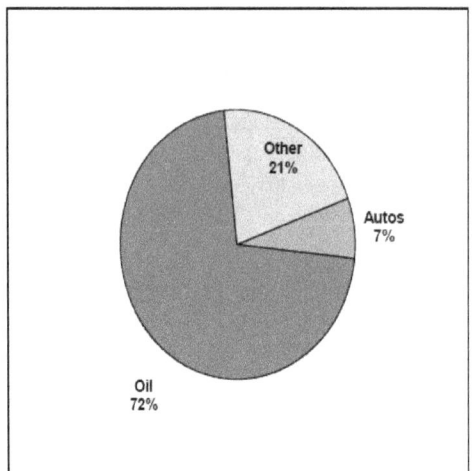

Figure 8. FTZ Foreign Input Levels, 1993 & 2012

(in $Billions of Current $, & Constant $1993)

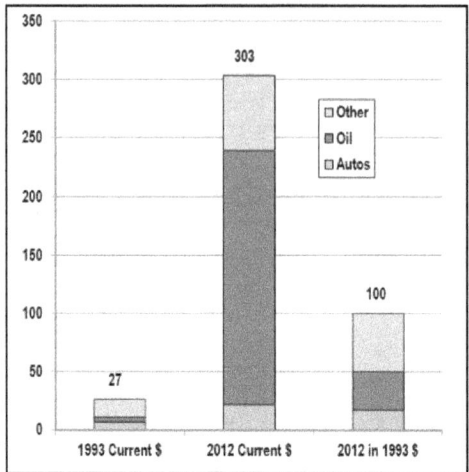

Source: USITC Dataweb.

Notes: For **Figure 8**, Data for each sector of the right hand bar were deflated using the Commerce Department's National income and Product Accounts Table 4.2.4 Price Indexes for Exports and Imports of Goods and Services by Type of Product. Data include foreign inputs into FTZs and bonded warehouses.

Overall Economic Benefits and Costs of FTZs

FTZs primarily benefit some manufacturing firms and potentially could benefit the economy as a whole with their savings possibilities. Savings from tariff reduction, administrative efficiencies, tax benefits, and duty deferral may help U.S. corporations maintain operations in the United States, and may attract foreign producers to establish manufacturing facilities in the United States. In turn, this could help communities hold onto their manufacturing bases and secondary service sector support systems and the jobs that go with them. Consumers may benefit from any cost savings that may be passed along. Federal, state, and local tax revenues may benefit from increased activity that the FTZs may generate.

Balancing these benefits of zone use are four potential costs to the U.S. economy. First, granting tariff reductions on imported components might disadvantage *domestic producers of competing components* whose products would otherwise be somewhat protected by the tariffs. Second, if certain producers in an industry obtain zone status to save production costs, this could put *other domestic producers of the final products* in the same industry at a competitive disadvantage. Third, the tariff benefits companies enjoy by operating in FTZs can also result in some loss or deferral of tariff revenue for the United States, although U.S. tariffs are generally low and represent a very small share of government revenue.[21] Finally, some economists might argue that

---

[21] No estimates are available on the value of tariffs foregone each year because of FTZ use. However, tariffs are still payable on the share of FTZ imports that is ultimately entered into the United States for consumption. In FY2010, according to the U.S. Customs and Border Protection, the duties payable on $209 billion dollars' worth of imports through U.S. FTZs was $1.1 billion.

FTZs result in a market distortion—a misallocation of resources to benefit a small number of businesses, especially oil companies. This issue is explored in greater detail in the "Current FTZ and Worldwide Zone-Related Issues for Congress" section.

FTZ regulations try to avoid potential "costs" of the FTZ program through the FTZ application procedures. The application process, administered by the FTZ Board, is explained in greater detail later in this section.

Business Benefits and Costs of FTZ Status

Specific benefits of zones for individual corporations producing in zones come from the law itself and the regulations implementing it. Costs come from administrative requirements involved in applying for and achieving zone status, monitoring of zones by the Customs and Border Protection, and reporting requirements by the U.S. FTZ Board. There are no precise estimates of the actual market value of the potential costs and benefits of FTZs in the United States or trade zones worldwide.

Benefits

Text Box 3 describes seven potential benefits for companies using FTZs. Most of the financial benefits come from three of the seven sources: duty reduction on inverted tariff situations, customs inventory control efficiencies, and duty exemption on exports. Other benefits include duty deferral, drawback elimination, tax savings, quota storage, and zone-to-zone transfer. Overall profits from FTZ use result from the combination of tiny savings per unit and high volume production.

> **Sources of Cost Savings for U.S. Foreign-Trade Zone Users**
> (Text Box 3)
>
> **Duty reduction on Inverted Tariff Situations:** With specific authority, zone users may choose the lower duty rate when a product is entered into customs territory (for importation) in inverted tariff situations (when the tariff rate on foreign inputs is higher than the tariff rate applied to the finished product produced in the zone).
>
> **Duty Deferral:** Cash flow savings can result because customs duties are paid only when and if the goods are transferred from the zone to U.S. customs territory for consumption.
>
> **Duty Exemption on Exports:** No duty is payable on goods which are exported from a zone or which are scrapped or destroyed in a zone.
>
> **Duty Drawback Elimination:** Zones eliminate the need for duty drawback. That is, the refunding of duties previously paid on imported and then re-exported merchandise.
>
> **Tax Savings:** Goods stored in zones and goods exported are not subject to state and local ad valorem taxes, such as personal property taxes, where applicable.
>
> **Zone-to-Zone Transfer:** Zones can transfer merchandise "in-bond" (i.e., insured) from one zone to another. Customs duties may be deferred until the product's eventual entry into U.S. customs territory.
>
> **Customs Inventory Control Efficiencies:** Cost savings (especially cash-flow savings) can occur from zone efficiencies affecting inventory control. These efficiencies include customs procedures such as direct delivery and weekly entries.
>
> **Source:** U.S. Foreign-Trade Zones Board.

Duty Reduction on Inverted Tariff Situations. Of all FTZ benefits, "duty reduction on inverted tariff situations" is generally the one most heavily used by businesses. It likely accounts for more than 50% of the total money saved from zone use, according to the FTZ Board.[22] Duty reduction on imports results because FTZ users can typically choose to pay either the tariff level that

---

[22] This estimate is made by the FTZ Board based on information contained in new zone and subzone applications. Calculating actual savings would require more extensive reporting on the part of zone users.

applies to the imported components, or that which applies to the finished goods.[23] Savings can be considerable. A new Volkswagen production plant in Chattanooga, TN, that recently won FTZ status estimated that it could save $1.9 million, or $13 per car in inverted tariff savings, on producing 150,000 cars annually.[24] In the oil industry, most inverted tariff benefits accrue to just a small sector—the petrochemical industry, which accounts for about 15% to 17% of total refinery yield.[25] Due to the potential impact on domestic suppliers, prior FTZ Board authorization is required for these types of savings. There are no independent estimates of the cost savings derived from the FTZs.

Customs and Inventory Efficiencies. Customs and inventory efficiencies, especially those obtained through "bundling" of entries (which are reports of individual shipments of goods entering or leaving zones), are another significant source of savings for FTZ users. In addition to time and paperwork savings, "bundling" allows an importer to file an entry for an entire week and pay a single merchandise processing fee (up to $485) instead of a separate entry and merchandise processing fee for each shipment. In this way, large-operation zone users can cut their processing fees by about 90%.[26] The National Association of Foreign Trade Zones (NAFTZ) estimates that FTZs handle more than 10% of U.S. imports each year in terms of dollar value, but account for less than 1% of the actual number of import filings made with Customs and Border Protection (CBP), because of "bundling." For a large company with 10 warehouses across the United States, each with several hundred deliveries per week, for example, bundling efficiencies could mean a reduction in processing fees from roughly "$2 million a year to about $25,000 per year."[27]

Duty Exemption. Merchandise can be re-exported from a zone without the payment of duties, providing another significant source of savings to U.S. exporters. In addition, no duty is payable on goods that are imported into zones and ultimately consumed, scrapped, or destroyed in the

---

[23] If the importer elects to pay the tariff rate as it would apply to the imported component, he claims "privileged" status; If he elects to pay the tariff rate as it would apply to the finished product, he claims "non-privileged" status. Example: If an importer claims "privileged status" on carburetors and fan belts entered into zones for incorporation into cars, then he would pay the "carburetors" and "fan belt," tariff rates, respectively, on the imported value of these components when the auto actually leaves the zone. If he claims "non-privileged status," he would pay the tariff rate applicable to the finished auto on the combined value of the carburetor and the belts when the finished auto exits the zone.

[24] *Volkswagen Could Save Nearly $2 million a Year in Tariffs*, Timesfreepress.com, March 19, 2011.

[25] Tariffs on crude oil depend on whether it is refined inside or outside FTZs, and whether or not it enters the United States under a free trade agreement or applicable trade preference program: If crude oil is refined in the United States, but not in FTZs, producers would pay the applicable tariff on the total value of the crude oil when it enters the United States (10.5 cents or 5.25 cents per barrel, depending on the crude oil), and then refine it to make the products—gasoline, diesel, kerosene, jet fuel, and petrochemicals. If crude oil is refined in the United States, but not in FTZs, and enters under a free trade agreement or trade preference program which exempts crude oil from tariffs, such as the Africa under the African Growth and Opportunity Act, no tariffs are payable. If, instead, crude oil is brought into the United States through FTZs, producers would first make gasoline, diesel, kerosene, and jet fuel from it and then pay the tariff on that share of the crude oil that went into these final products. They would not need to pay any tariff on the part of the crude oil that became petrochemicals, since no tariffs are payable on petrochemicals.

[26] Merchandise processing fees (MPFs) are a percentage of the value of imported goods (0.3464%), but cannot exceed $485. Thus, the single weekly entry reduces MPFs for companies whose weekly imports are valued at greater than $140,011.55—the amount required to get charged the maximum fee. U.S. Customs and Border Protection, "User fee - Merchandise Processing Fees," https://help.cbp.gov/app/answers/detail/a_id/334/~/user-fee---merchandise-processing-fees.

[27] This estimate is based on CRS calculations of possible configurations that could lead to the savings quoted. The quote is from a spokesperson for Hillwood Properties, a real estate developer known for its FTZ development and management work around the Fort Worth Texas, in *American Shipper*, op. cit, p. 44.

---

zone. For example, damaged packages or broken bottles can be removed from shipments of packaged or bottled goods.[28]

Costs

According to the FTZ Board, the costs of FTZ use, and the "red tape" involved in order to take advantage of zone opportunities, can be substantial. Therefore, companies need to weigh carefully potential costs and benefits of zone use before applying for FTZ status. There are startup costs and maintenance costs. Because of this, according to an FTZ trade interest group, FTZs work best when a company can potentially see a return of 100% to 200% on investment in zone use. If the investment return is smaller, it may not be worth the startup and continuing costs.[29]

Startup costs include (1) the application process (detailed in the next section);[30] (2) background checks for importers; (3) a physical security system—usually a fenced-in system with locks, guards, and cameras; (4) an inventory control system and related software to track the movement of products (which must be in place before CBP officially activates the operation); and (5) consultants, for those who prefer their assistance in setting up and managing a zone.

Maintenance costs after full zone status is in effect include (1) greater oversight by CBP officials;[31] (2) at least one full-time person to manage a zone; (3) a "bond" payment, which is held by the government as a guarantee against potential tariffs owed on products in FTZs;[32] and (4) annual fees by grantees for zone use. The FTZ Act requires zone grantees to operate zones as public utilities, but grantees are able to charge zone users for costs associated with managing the zone. Fees for zone users range from several thousand dollars up to $10,000 or more a year.[33]

The Administrative Mechanism Behind FTZs[34]

Several U.S. agencies are involved in administering the FTZ program. The FTZ Board is responsible for the establishment, maintenance, and administration of zones under the FTZ Act. The FTZ Board consists of two members: the Secretary of Commerce and the Secretary of the Treasury. The Secretary of Commerce is the chairman and executive officer, and appoints the

---

[28] U.S. Department of Homeland Security, Customs and Border Protection, *Importing into the United States; A Guide for Commercial Importers*, p. 153.

[29] *American Shipper*, IT in FTZ, op. cit., p. 44.

[30] Recent regulations have shortened the process for manufacturing authorizations from 1 year to 4 months, if no issues are raised. In such cases, FTZ sites can be designated in as little as 30 days. The FTZ Board is available to help applicants with the complexities of applying.

[31] Without zone status, the product is initially cleared when the entry and customs documents are filed. However, for products entered into zones, there is a constant opportunity for CBP monitoring, especially when items enter or leave a zone. Even if the product is not in an FTZ, however, companies may still be liable for CBP audits, and may have to pay additional duties (i.e., anti-dumping or countervailing duties) well after a product has been imported. What is different in an FTZ is that there is an extra layer of CBP oversight to make sure, for example, that the components or the finished products do not enter the commerce of the United States before applicable duties are paid. All importers also have to pay single or continuous bonds to ensure payment of customs duties.

[32] The cost of bond can be as high as $100,000 on large or high value operations.

[33] A grantee is typically a city, county, or economic development authority operating the zone in the public interest. A grantee is responsible for uniform treatment for zone users.

[34] U.S. Department of Homeland Security, *U.S. Customs and Border Protection, Foreign-Trade Zones Manual*, various pages.

executive secretary (chief operating officer) of the FTZ Board, who is supported by a professional staff of seven. The Secretary of the Treasury's responsibilities relate to the protection of the revenue as well as tariff and trade policy considerations.

The Department of Homeland Security's Customs and Border Protection (CBP) acts as an advisor to the FTZ Board and is responsible for direct oversight of zone activity and ensuring compliance with the FTZ Act and all laws and regulations pertaining to zone use. CBP is responsible for activating FTZs, securing them, controlling dutiable merchandise moving into and out of them, and protecting and collecting the revenue. CBP is also responsible for ensuring that there is no evasion or violation of U.S. laws and regulations governing imported and exported merchandise, and ensuring that the zones program is free from terrorist activity. To this end, CBP, which is not normally onsite at the zones, must sign off on every shipment into and out of a zone. CBP also provides audits and compliance reviews of zone activity, including oversight of safeguards for checking container seals and other security measures. Homeland Security's Bureau of Immigration and Customs Enforcement (ICE) is involved in a voluntary partnership with companies in FTZs to combat unlawful employment, although the same immigration and labor laws apply in FTZs as in any other U.S. location.[35]

Other agencies involved in the oversight of zone shipments include the Department of Agriculture and the U.S. Food and Drug Administration.

Application for FTZ Status

The FTZ Board does not own or operate any zones. Rather, it provides grants of authority to applicants to establish, operate, and maintain zones. Once a zone has been established, the organization that applied for the zone is known as the "grantee." Grantees are public or private corporations that manage a zone locally. They provide and maintain facilities in connection with the zone according to regulations established by the FTZ Board. Under FTZ regulations, they are required to operate the zones as public utilities, with fair and reasonable rates, make annual reports to the FTZ Board on their activities, and provide uniform treatment under like conditions to zone users.

On February 28, 2012, the U.S. FTZ Board published in the *Federal Register*[36] the first major set of revisions to U.S. FTZ regulations since 1991. They were issued in part as a continuing response to congressional oversight and issues identified by the House Ways and Means Committee in 1989.[37]

While the new regulations address a variety of issues, they were designed primarily to streamline the application process for manufacturers and distributors who want to operate in an FTZ or establish a subzone. Currently, a company can obtain FTZ designation for its facility in as little as 30 days, although up to a five-month process may be required in certain circumstances. The five-month process is still a significant reduction from the 10 to 12 months that would have been required in the past. The revised regulations also reduce the timeline for applications for

---

[35] U.S. Department of Homeland Security, *FTZ Manual*, op. cit., various pages.

[36] 15 CFR Part 400.

[37] For previous discussion on issues raised, see archived CRS Report RL30268, *U.S. Foreign-Trade Zones: Current Issues*, by Mary Jane Bolle, p. 9.

production authority from 12 months to 4 months (120 days), in part by reducing the amount of information required in many instances. If issues are raised by concerned parties during the 120-day application process, the applicant must then follow a lengthier in-depth procedure, similar to what was required in the past. Major differences between old and new procedures are summarized in **Text Box 4** (below).

Old and New Simplified Procedures for FTZ Production Authority
(Text Box 4)

New Procedures

New, simplified regulations set up a 120-day (approximately four-month) timeline for all new applications to set up manufacturing operations inside FTZs. Under the new procedures, fewer types of information are required to be submitted. Required information includes

 (1) the name of the company;
 (2) a summary of the activity; and
 (3) a list of imported components and finished products.

After the application is submitted to the FTZ Board, the executive secretary appoints an examiner who checks the application, posts it on the FTZ Board website, and opens a comment period so all interested parties (government, industry specialists, and other non-governmental organizations) can respond to any "public interest" issues. That is, any concerns that the FTZ would not be in the public interest could be raised at this time. Because the FTZ Board is small, the comments received are very important in the review process. To supplement this information, the examiner may also consult industry specialists in government and consider the result of prior application in the industry. The examiner prepares a report with recommendations to the FTZ Board. Approval may be subject to specific restrictions to allow or limit certain activities to avoid a negative impact on domestic suppliers or competitors. If issues are raised, applications can be subject to the more stringent 12-month process (below).

Old Procedures (Still Used If Issues are Raised in the 120-Day Production Review Process)

These procedures (which take about one year to conclude) require the applying company to show how the proposed manufacturing activity would contribute to the U.S. economy through job creation or other means. Applicants would be required to provide information on "economic factors" including:

 (1) employment impact;
 (2) exports and re-exports;
 (3) retention or creation of manufacturing or processing activity;
 (4) extent of value-added activity;
 (5) effect on import levels of relevant products;
 (6) foreign competition in relevant products;
 (7) impact on related domestic industry; and
 (8) technology transfers and investment effects (15 CFR §400.31(b)(2)).

The FTZ Board would then undertake a detailed analysis to determine whether allowing a manufacturing activity would displace or cause harm to an existing U.S. company.

Source: Summarized from material included on the FTZ Board website.

Current FTZ and Worldwide Zone-Related Issues for Congress[38]

Current zone-related issues for Congress reflect the supply-chain role of free trade zones in a complex, increasingly integrated world. Congressional issues have both U.S. and worldwide aspects. Domestic issues include whether FTZs represent a misallocation of U.S. resources; whether data relating to zone use are sufficient; and the extent to which U.S. FTZ zone use affects U.S. employment and the competitiveness of U.S. firms. Internationally, congressional issues relate to the effectiveness of trade zones worldwide as a tool for economic development and global competitiveness and U.S. influence on worker rights issues in zones around the world through trade policy.

Do U.S. FTZs Encourage a Misallocation of U.S. Resources?

As noted above, the U.S. FTZ system was established in the 1930s with the goal of spurring U.S. commerce in the wake of the Great Depression and the high tariff regime established by the Smoot-Hawley Tariff Act. Today, U.S. tariff levels are among the lowest in the world and U.S. commerce is highly connected with the global economy. Given the changes that have occurred since its passage, Congress may choose to consider whether the FTZ system today still fulfills the original intent of the FTZ Act and furthermore, if it remains the best vehicle through which to do so.

From a theoretical standpoint, efficiencies that reduce the cost of production increase productivity and benefit the overall economy—more is produced with less. When the FTZ system provides such gains in productivity to U.S. firms, the U.S. economy benefits. A problem may arise, however, to the extent that these FTZ benefits are not available to all U.S. producers. As with any system that confers specific benefits to some but not all producers in an economy, the FTZ system may cause a misallocation of productive resources. These potential distortions could be avoided by simply providing FTZ benefits to all U.S. firms. Though only a fraction of U.S. firms utilize the FTZ system, no firms are excluded from applying for FTZ status and hence the benefits are technically available to all U.S. firms. In reality, this may not be the case. As mentioned above, given the high startup costs associated with FTZ use, the system is most likely to benefit large firms with a high volume of production. The FTZ Board has tried to address some of these concerns regarding the accessibility of the program by simplifying its application procedure.

If the ultimate goal is a greater reduction in U.S. tariffs, FTZs provide one, if not the most efficient, way to do so. Tariffs themselves can cause a misallocation of resources, and though economic theory would suggest the U.S. economy benefits when tariffs are eliminated, such action may be politically infeasible. Companies in import-sensitive industries may be negatively

---

[38] Historical material in this and the following two sections is drawn from: U.S. General Accounting Office, *Foreign-Trade Zone Growth Primarily Benefits Users Who Import For Domestic Commerce;* GAO/GGD 84-52, March 2, 1984, and *Foreign-Trade Zones Program Needs Clarified Criteria,* GAO/NSIAD 899-85; U.S. International Trade Commission, *The Implications of Foreign-Trade Zones for U.S. Industries and for Competitive Conditions Between U.S. and Foreign Firms,* USITC Publication 1496, February, 1984; *The Implications of Foreign-Trade Zones for U.S. Industries and for Competitive Conditions Between U.S. and Foreign Firms,* USITC Publication 2059, February, 1988; and *U.S. Foreign-Trade Zones Act,* 19 U.S.C. 812-81u.

impacted by the reduction of tariffs and may have a strong incentive to maintain tariff protection. The FTZ system and its application process, which allows for public comment, provides a mechanism by which tariffs are, in effect, lowered only in industries without strong domestic opposition. Given that tariff rates in the United States are not equal across products, it is unclear whether lowering one specific tariff line would create more or less distortion. Congress could more efficiently provide tariff free access to the U.S. market by an across the board cut of tariff rates, which would guarantee equal access by all U.S. firms. Such broad-based tariff reductions have typically occurred in the United States through multilateral trade liberalization negotiations in the World Trade Organization (WTO).[39]

Like the specific tariff benefits, one could also argue that the logistical benefits provided by FTZ use create distortions. FTZ users benefit from more streamlined customs procedures and lower merchandise processing fees, while those outside zones do not. Again, the question arises as to whether the program is truly accessible. Merchandise processing fees are based on a percentage of the total import value, but are subject to a cap. Larger importers would reach that cap more quickly and have a stronger incentive to pay the upfront costs of establishing an FTZ.

Broader customs reform applicable to all importers could provide similar benefits without the risk of distortions. But, given the background checks and heightened security associated with operating an FTZ, providing all firms with the logistical benefits of FTZ use may not be feasible. CBP has discussed permitting importers to file one entry form per month, regardless of whether the company has FTZ status, as part of a "simplified summary" process.[40] However, this proposal has reportedly run into logistical problems relating to the actual implementation of such a system across the broad spectrum of U.S. importers. Even if the vast majority of importers are deemed to be low risk, the sheer number of total importers means that even a small percent of high risk companies would involve a huge resource burden to ensure compliance. Ensuring the safety and security of U.S. imports in a cost-effective manner, while also facilitating timely trade, remains an ongoing challenge.

Data Availability Issues Relating to FTZs

Every shipment into and out of foreign-trade zones must be authorized by CBP. The documents that a company submits to CBP include the classification, country of origin, and the value of the merchandise. While this information is provided to CBP for every shipment and used by CBP to maintain oversight of the zone activity, this level of information is not publicly available. Public reports tracking the identity of products moving into and out of zones are incomplete, although two agencies publish data relating to FTZs. The Commerce Department (Bureau of the Census) publishes data on imports (foreign products) entered into zones. The U.S. FTZ Board publishes data on both foreign and domestic products entered into zones, and final products leaving zones for U.S. consumption and for export, respectively. The two agencies produce some estimates of zone use from different sources using different methods. While their final estimates are reasonably close on certain measurements, other data pertaining to FTZ use are lacking for both groups. (See **Table 1**, which compares data from the two sources and identifies missing data.)

---

[39] Prior to the establishment of the WTO, these negotiations were part of the General Agreement on Tariffs and Trade (GATT).

[40] U.S. CBP, *Simplified Process Fact Sheet*, August 2011; and CBP, *Simplified Entry Briefing*, April 2012.

Missing data, more importantly than slightly inconsistent data, can complicate policy recommendations.

Table 1. FTZ and Census Data Reported on Merchandise Entering or Leaving FTZs

	FTZ Data	Census Data
Reported Data on Merchandise Entering FTZs	• Summary values are reported for all merchandise received in zones, including both domestic and foreign status zone inputs. • Foreign status inputs are further disaggregated by type of product—but not by HTS code.	• Detailed data are published by HTS code and by country, on general imports into FTZs or bonded warehouses. Domestic components entering FTZs to be combined with foreign inputs are not tracked. • Data on general import charges (e.g., tariffs) are reported.
Reported Data on Merchandise Leaving FTZs	• Summary values for U.S. exports and shipments to the U.S. market are reported, but they only include the value of the material inputs (both domestic and foreign).	• Data on completed goods exiting FTZs for import into the United States or for export are not typically made public, but may be obtained by request for a special Census Bureau data run.
No Data are Reported Publicly on:	• HTS numbers of any foreign inputs. • Industry identification of any products leaving FTZs for import into or export from the United States. • Merchandise transferred between zones. • Tariffs—paid, payable, or avoided.	• Domestic inputs into zones. • Goods transferred from one zone to another. • The HTS relationship (or lack thereof) between foreign status products ("imports") entering zones and products leaving zones for U.S. customs territory and/or for export.

Source: For FTZ data: U.S. Foreign-Trade Zones Board Report to Congress, (various years); for Census data: USITC Dataweb, and interviews with Census and FTZ Board representatives.

The FTZ Board collects its data from zone users and publishes in its *Annual Report to Congress* summary data on "foreign" and "domestic status" inputs into FTZs later shipped to the United States or exported to places abroad. It also publishes more detailed industry-level data, specifically for foreign status inputs.[41]

The Census Bureau collects its data from importers and exporters, tracking the movement of products into or out of the United States in general.[42] For FTZs in particular, Census publishes detailed data by Harmonized Tariff Schedule (HTS) codes on imports into FTZs and bonded warehouses, along with data on import charges owed on these imports.[43] While Census does not regularly publish data by HTS code on merchandise that leaves FTZs for consumption in the United States, or for export, these data may be obtained upon special request.

Neither the FTZ Board nor the Census Bureau collects or publishes industry-specific data on (1) domestic inputs into zones; (2) goods transferred from zone to zone; (3) value added in zones; or

---

[41] No FTZ data are included on value added when these inputs are declared exported from zones, as mentioned below.

[42] Separate forms track: (1) merchandise imported into the United States; (2) merchandise shipped into an FTZ; (3) merchandise leaving a zone (whether exported, transferred from one zone to another; or transferred out of a zone for entry and domestic consumption); and (4) final reporting on imports and tariffs owed on imported goods. CBP form numbers are: for (1) 3461; (2) 214; (3) 7512; and (4) 7501.

[43] Data are published on the USITC Dataweb.

(4) the relationship between the actual character of goods entering and goods exiting FTZs. These data are reported by companies to CBP and are used for protecting the revenue, ensuring compliance with U.S. laws and regulations, and ensuring the secure movement of merchandise in the United States. However, they are not available publicly for other uses.

Security Issues Relating to FTZs

Security issues relating to imports are a continuing concern for CBP. The agency undertakes periodic reviews of companies, including companies bringing goods into and out of FTZs, along with the products they transport and process. CBP has reportedly developed a complex targeting system in its continuing effort to balance competing goals of facilitating trade, providing port security, and collecting trade revenues.[44]

Compared to products that are imported for consumption directly into the United States, FTZs incorporate additional screening and security measures. Unlike other imports, companies must apply to CBP to use a zone. Part of that process, known as "activation," includes a background check on key employees, a review of the security of the facility, and assessing the integrity of the inventory control and recordkeeping system. A company must also produce a detailed procedures manual explaining how all merchandise is handled at every stage of its movement through the zone. The storage of merchandise in a zone exposes that merchandise to audit and inspection for the length of time that it remains within the zone, often significantly longer than if it had been entered and cleared into commerce upon arrival at a U.S. port.

In 2007, the Senate Finance Committee requested the Government Accountability Office (GAO) to undertake a review of trade and security concerns related to CBP's "in-bond cargo" system. Shipments to, from, and between zones are one portion of the in-bond system, and these concerns relate to the in-bond system in general, not exclusively to the FTZ process.[45] The GAO's findings concluded that although the in-bond system is designed to facilitate the flow of trade, CBP cannot assess the extent of the program's use because it collects little information on in-bond shipments and performs limited analysis of data that it does collect. GAO further concluded that limited information on in-bond cargo "impedes CBP efforts to manage security risks and ensure proper targeting of inspections." As a result, some higher risk cargo may not be identified for inspection, and scarce inspection resources may be used for some lower-risk cargo.[46] CBP is taking steps to automate the in-bond system to address the concerns. While concerns have been raised regarding the in-bond shipment process, similar concerns have not applied directly to the FTZ process. The movement of goods into and out of U.S. zones is automated and available for security and tracking purposes.

---

[44] Government Accountability Office (GAO), Report to the Committee on Finance, U.S. Senate, *International Trade: Persistent Weaknesses in the In-Bond Cargo System Impede Customs and Border Protection's Ability to Address Revenue, Trade, and Security Concerns*, April, 2007, and discussions with representatives from the Census Bureau.

[45] Ibid, p. 1. In-bond shipments are those not intended to enter U.S. commerce, and therefore import duties and taxes are not required of them. "Bond" is an insurance payment required by CBP to cover U.S. duties listed on the Harmonized Tariff Schedule in case the goods are lost, misdirected, or fail to arrive at the FTZ, bonded warehouse, or port of export. Bonded cargo carried in sealed containers is said to be "in bond." Cargo is typically transferred "in bond" from ports of entry into zones, out of zones to ports of exports, and from zone to zone. The Customs form required to accompany the merchandise (form 214) requires little information on the contents of the in-bond cargo.

[46] GAO report, op. cit., inside cover.

Another security assessment involving zones globally was undertaken by an international inter-governmental group, the Financial Action Task Force (FATF)/Organization for Economic Cooperation and Development (OECD).[47] Its findings are reported in *Money Laundering Vulnerabilities of Free Trade Zones*, a report released in March of 2010. Two of its case studies identified smuggling and tax evasion activities involving a U.S. company and a U.S. FTZ, respectively. Final recommendations in the report did not differentiate between those for zones in the world at large and those relating to U.S. FTZs. However, they focused, among other things, on the factors which could remedy weaknesses in both groups, including (1) improvement in systems relating to the collection, quality, and international exchange of trade data; (2) greater use of electronic customs filing and reporting systems with universally compatible data fields; and (3) licensing, regulating, and monitoring of entities acting as customs brokers and persons operating bonded warehouses.[48]

U.S. Employment and Global Competitiveness Impact of FTZs

Proponents of FTZs continually point to their job-creating and trade-creating potential. FTZs employ 320,000 mostly manufacturing workers in the United States. This represents less than 3% of total U.S. manufacturing employment.[49]

Nevertheless, factors affecting U.S. employment in small ways are of interest to Congress. Since 1979, the number of manufacturing jobs in the United States has declined by nearly 40%, while output has more than doubled.[50] Most analysts agree that two factors have contributed to this decline: (1) productivity gains in domestic operations; and (2) movement of U.S. manufacturing facilities abroad due to lower operating costs. Considerable debate, however, persists over which of these factors has had a greater influence, and how to improve the situation.

FTZ trade groups argue that FTZ operations can encourage job retention and job growth. More broadly, advocates argue that FTZ use enhances the global competiveness of firms located in the United States. They argue that importers can, in some cases, save production and transportation costs by setting up new final assembly operations in U.S. FTZs or by gaining FTZ designation for existing plants.[51] For example, in the automotive industry, Nissan estimates that annual FTZ benefits, net of the additional costs of operating an FTZ site, can be as much as $8.3 million a year.[52] The company argues that without the FTZ benefits it might move U.S. production to other countries, though such a decision would likely also depend on a number of other factors, perhaps more significant than FTZ status. As with the ongoing debate regarding the drop in manufacturing

---

[47] This study was produced jointly by the FATF and OECD in Paris. The Financial Action Task Force FATF was established by the G-7 Summit in Paris in 1989 as an inter-governmental body to develop a coordinated international response to mounting concern over money laundering and terrorist financing. It consists of 36 members: 34 countries and two regional organizations (the Gulf Cooperation Council and the European Commission), and 31 international and regional Associate Members or Observers who also participate in its work.

[48] FATF/OECD, *Money Laundering Vulnerabilities of Free Trade Zones*, March 2010, case studies 3, p. 21, 9, p. 26, and recommendations, p. 37.

[49] U.S. manufacturing employment, itself, represents only 9% of total employment.

[50] See *Economic Report of the President, 2012*, Table B-46 and B-13.

[51] See, for example, *American Shipper*, IT in FTZ, op. cit., p. 44.

[52] Nissan North America, Inc., *Nissan North America, Inc. - A Foreign Trade Zone Success Story*, Presentation at House of Representatives Manufacturing Caucus-Foreign Trade Zones: A Home Run for Trade and Jobs, June 2012.

---

employment, determining whether any specific action causes net job growth or loss is challenging, particularly because these actions often have direct as well as indirect effects.

Effectiveness of World Trade Zones as a Tool for Economic Development

As noted above (see "Growth of Free Trade Zones Worldwide"), the United States has been involved in promoting free trade zones worldwide through a number of different avenues. Some might argue that world export processing zones and a focus on exports do not necessarily contribute to economic development. Economists argue that export-led growth works best as a development tool when the world economy is growing quickly. They point out that it works less well when world economic growth (led by consumers in developed, high-import countries) slows. In such a case, export-led growth can be cyclical and destabilizing. Therefore, developing a domestic economy that depends more on domestic consumer demand adds an element of stability that could benefit developing countries over the long run.

Others may argue that an initial lack of strong domestic demand is precisely why countries may benefit from a focus on exports in the early stages of development. The specific goods a developing country is most efficient in producing may be not be demanded domestically or not at the scale necessary to achieve maximum efficiency. Hence, some argue that economic development may occur much faster with export processing zones than without them. In addition to the tariff benefits, the infrastructure components of zones attract foreign investment that might not otherwise occur. The challenge, however, as growth begins, is for a country to (1) continually diversify into producing higher value-added goods; (2) find ways to continually upgrade the skills of the workforce to produce those goods; and (3) encourage domestic consumption of some of the goods produced in zones. Countries that have followed this model by government planning toward this goal have been most successful.[53]

Some economists also argue that it would be more efficient and less market distorting to work within the WTO to eliminate tariffs worldwide to help promote international economic development than to continue to promote export processing zones. While this may be true, history has shown that the process of eliminating tariffs is very slow, and while this would solve the issue of differing tariffs across countries, it does not speak to the infrastructure and customs simplification benefits of free trade zones in developing countries. Some may argue that a greater focus in the WTO and other international organizations on trade capacity building and ensuring that developing countries have the means to process, track, and transport traded goods could help with this ongoing challenge. The Doha Development Agenda, the current round of multilateral talks in the WTO, has included negotiations on potential disciplines in trade facilitation and capacity building, although the overall Doha Agenda has been stalled in recent years.[54]

---

[53] Such countries include Mexico, Taiwan, Singapore, and South Korea. Export processing zones are also more successful where a substantial share of the operations are jointly owned by foreign and domestic companies. They have not been as successful in promoting economic development in countries where there is civil conflict, corruption, war, or other political, labor, or social instability. ILO, *Economic and social Effects of Multinational Enterprises in Export Processing Zones*, p. 24 and 31; the Flagstaff Institute, *The Role of EPZs in the Era of Regulated Trade*, p. 29-32.

[54] For more information on the Doha Development Agenda, see CRS Report RL32060, *World Trade Organization Negotiations: The Doha Development Agenda*, by Ian F. Fergusson.

Trade Zones Worldwide and Worker Rights

Congress has an impact on worker rights in trade zones worldwide through U.S. trade preference laws and free trade agreements. Trade preference laws traditionally require, among other things, that as a condition of continued eligibility for trade benefits, countries must be taking steps to afford their workers "internationally recognized worker rights."[55] Almost all U.S. free trade agreements include language pledging to uphold a similar list of worker rights, and all but three of the agreements[56] include language stating that Parties agree not to "waive or derogate from" their statutes or regulations in order to attract trade with and/or investment by the other Party.[57]

However, there may be a grey area on the applicability of the trade preference program and free trade agreement provisions to free trade zones, at least under some free trade agreements. While the United States has suspended trade preferences to certain countries because of labor violations,[58] the applicability of labor provisions in free trade agreements specifically to trade zones in other countries has never been tested under dispute resolution procedures.[59]

Depending on laws of a specific country, zones could be an unclear area for labor requirements under free trade zones. One U.S. free trade agreement partner country, Jordan, in the past, permitted relaxed labor standards in its free trade zones. The fact that Jordan had different labor standards in its free trade zones than in other parts of its country came to light in 2006, when a watchdog organization, the National Labor Committee, published a report documenting problematical labor conditions in Jordan's free trade zones.[60] The case was eventually handled through discussions between U.S. and Jordanian labor representatives, and Jordan took a number of steps to eliminate the problems. Since this case was handled informally, it did not establish a precedent to address labor standards in the free trade zones of countries with which the United States has free trade agreements. Whether the issue of labor standards in free trade zones will be addressed in future trade agreements is not known.[61]

---

[55] "Internationally recognized worker rights" are defined in the Trade Act of 1974, as amended, as: (a) the right of association; (b) the right to organize and bargain collectively; (c) a prohibition on the use of any form of forced or compulsory labor; (d) protections for child labor, including the "worst forms of child labor," and (e) acceptable conditions of work with respect to minimum wages, hours of work, and occupational safety and health.

[56] These include the U.S.-Israel Free Trade Agreement, the U.S.-Canada Free Trade Agreement, and the North American Free Trade Agreement, which superseded it, for Canada.

[57] Language to this effect is included in free trade agreements with at least 16 countries. In four of these agreements, with Peru, Colombia, Panama, and South Korea, such language is enforceable under the agreement's dispute resolution procedures.

[58] Myanmar (Burma), for example, is one such country.

[59] In most U.S. free trade agreements, the term "territory" in the definitions section, is typically defined to include "exclusive economic zone" (which, itself, is not further defined in the agreements). However, in the labor chapters, the word "territory" is typically used in provisions that are not generally designated as enforceable through the dispute resolution procedures provisions. In the most recent free trade agreements with Peru, Colombia, South Korea, and Panama, the first time the word "territory" appears is in the section on labor cooperation and trade capacity building.

[60] Jordan's free trade zones are called qualifying industrial zones, or QIZs. They were created under the Qualifying Industrial Zone trade preference program created by a 1996 amendment to the U.S.-Israel Free Trade Agreement, and have continued under a U.S. free trade Agreement with Jordan, approved by Congress in 2001. The report was: National Labor Committee, *U.S.-Jordan Free Trade Agreement Descends into Human Trafficking and Involuntary Servitude*, May, 2006, 161 p.

[61] Reportedly, the U.S. Trans Pacific Partnership Agreement (TPP) proposal would describe what partner countries would need to do to adopt and maintain ILO core labor principles the principles. It reportedly would "clarify" that TPP countries must apply their national labor laws in export processing zones and free trade zones. World Trade Online, (continued...)

International organizations have issued guidelines addressing labor issues in free trade zones, to varying degrees. For example, WTO rules and good practices on export policy do not address the issue of worker rights specifically.[62] At the 1996 WTO Singapore Ministerial, the WTO member countries voted to renew their commitment to the observance of internationally recognized core labor standards and named the ILO as the "competent body" to set and deal with these standards.[63] OECD Guidelines for Multinational Enterprises include labor guidelines. However, they do not mention export processing zones or free trade zones specifically.

The ILO has issued a number of reports on working conditions in export processing zones. None of them, however, is up-to-date in showing where specific country laws allow different labor standards in free trade zones. In a 2008 report, the ILO examined labor practices by multinational corporations in countries covered by free trade agreements. It found that such corporations unevenly implement their individual labor codes of conduct. It found that while labor conditions are sometimes better inside zones than in other sectors of the economy, poor working conditions in terms of overtime, occupational health and safety, wages, and freedom of association remain in many zones.[64]

Outlook: Future of U.S. FTZs and Zones Worldwide?

From time to time, concerns have arisen within the trade community about the future of free trade zones, including U.S. FTZs. Will they disappear with continuing trade liberalization and continuing reductions in tariffs?

The future role of zones in the global manufacturing supply chain largely depends on many as yet unknown and undetermined factors. For example, after the 1993 North American Free Trade Agreement (NAFTA) led to ultimate tariff elimination for trade among the United States, Mexico, and Canada, questions arose as to whether *maquiladoras*[65] along the U.S.-Mexican border would diminish in importance, and entire FTA partner countries would become, in essence vast "free trade zones" for trade with each other. Data since then, however, show that free trade zone use has remained popular in developing and developed countries alike because of its diverse benefits,

---

(...continued)

Inside U.S. Trade, "USTR Tables TPP Labor Proposal That Goes Beyond May 10 Template," January 5, 2012

[62] "WTO Rules and Good Practice on Export Policy," WTO Staff Working Paper TPRD9701.WPF.

[63] In the Singapore Declaration, WTO members: (1) affirmed their support for the ILO's work in promoting "internationally recognized core labor standards"—a list from Section 507 of the Trade Act of 1974 (P.L. 93-618) which is very similar to the list of ILO core labor principles, and includes: the right to organize and bargain collectively, protections against forced labor, protections for child labor, and labor standards relating to minimum wages, maximum hours, and safety and health protections; (2) believed that economic growth and development and further trade liberalization contribute to the promotion of these standards; (3) rejected the use of labor standards for protectionist purposes; (4) agreed that the comparative advantage of countries, particularly low-wage developing countries, must not be put into question; and (5) noted that the WTO and ILO Secretariats will continue their existing collaboration.

[64] ILO, *Economic Development and Working Conditions in Export Processing Zones: A Survey of Trends*, Working Paper by William Milberg and Matthew Amengual, Geneva, 2008, p.62.

[65] The word *maquiladora* is still used in Mexico, typically to denote foreign-owned operations.

---

and that, in fact, there are currently at least 3,700 firms employing at least 1.2 million workers in zones in Mexico.[66]

More than 15 years after these questions were voiced, export processing zones have continued to expand in terms of countries hosting them, corporations investing in them, and workers being hired to labor in them. Between 1997 and 2006, the number of free trade zones worldwide quadrupled, and the number of workers employed in them tripled. For FTZs in the United States, the direction of growth is the same as for world export processing zones, but the expansion has been more modest, with relatively little growth in employment. Between 1997 and 2012, the overall increase in zone use, along with the particular expansion by the oil sector, has resulted in a decrease in the number of firms using zones, (from 3,600 to 3,200). However, it has also resulted in an increase in employment (from 310,000 to 370,000) and a nearly four-fold increase in the current dollar value of merchandise received/shipped.[67] (See **Table A-2.**)

Reasons previously identified by the OECD as supporting the growth of world export processing zones as policy tools could continue: (1) the increasing emphasis on export-oriented growth; (2) the increasing emphasis on foreign direct investment-oriented growth; (3) the transfer of production of labor intensive industries from developed to developing countries; and (4) the growing international division of labor and incidence of global production networks.[68]

Major factors which, in the future, could increase the use of free trade zones around the world, including U.S. FTZs, are (1) continuing improvements in technology, which will extend recent advancements in communication tools, computer capabilities, and the transport industry; (2) advancements and improvements in security monitoring; (3) new efficiencies for zone users including advancements in automated, electronic tracking of goods and services traded internationally; and (4) external trends. Possible external trends that could give a significant boost to U.S. FTZs, specifically, could include those events or forces that would encourage a return of basic manufacturing to the United States and a boost to U.S. exports.

If all trade barriers and security issues were eliminated between all countries, exports and imports could move as easily among countries as between U.S. states. As a result, the need for the zones worldwide would be greatly diminished. However, as long as international tariff and non-tariff barriers remain, along with the need for heightened security to deal with issues such as terrorism and money laundering, the U.S. FTZ system and other zone programs abroad are likely to continue and even, possibly, expand.

---

[66] The ILO Database on Export Processing Zones (Revised), April, 2007, p. 13.

[67] These data from the U.S. FTZ Board reflect the total for domestic and foreign merchandise received, as contrasted with data in **Figures 7 and 8**, which reflect only foreign input levels.

[68] OECD, *Export Processing Zones: Past and Future Role in Trade and Development*, by Michael Engman, Osamu Onodera, and Enrico Pinali, OECD Trade Policy Working Paper, No. 53, 2007, p. 8.

Appendix.

Table A-1. U.S. FTZ Activity by Zone Type, 2012

| | Active FTZs | Active Manufacturing Operations | Total Merchandise Received | | Final Dispensation of FTZ Products ($Bil.) | |
			Foreign Inputs ($ Bil.)[a]	Domestic Inputs ($ Bil.)	Exported ($Bil.)[b]	Domestically Consumed/ "Imported" ($Bil.)[c]
TOTAL	174	276	$304	$429	$70	$662

Source: CRS analysis, from Foreign-Trade Zones Board, 74th Annual Report, August, 2013.

a. Foreign inputs excludes foreign-origin items that are duty-paid prior to entering the FTZ.

b. Exports and domestically consumed products do not include value added. They are based solely on material inputs.

c. May include some products previously held in warehouses in previous years.

How FTZs Function: Shipment of Goods Into and Out of FTZs
(Text Box A-1)

Ports of entry are the level at which Customs and Border Patrol (CBP) enforces import and export laws and regulations and implements immigration policies and programs. Entry of goods into a zone requires a permit from the port director and signature by the zone operator for its admission. An additional copy of the permit is transmitted to the Census Bureau.

For goods shipped into FTZs:

- When a shipment reaches the United States, the zone operator will request permission from CBP to move the goods into an FTZ.

- The port director then issues a permit for admission of the merchandise, and the merchandise enters the zone. No permit is needed for domestic status merchandise made in the United States.

- Customs and Border Protection (CBP) (generally electronically) reviews the application and supporting documents for completeness and to determine whether the application may be approved without physical examination of the merchandise, and approves the permit. CBP approves permits of admission for most low-risk shipments without examination.

For goods leaving FTZs:

- When merchandise exits the zone for official entry into the United States, or for export, two types of documents are required: (1) documents for release of merchandise: and (2) documents with information for duty assessment and for statistical purposes. Both can be filed electronically through the *Automated Broker Interface System* (ABI) of the *Automated Commercial System* (ACS).

- Similarly, when merchandise exits the zone for export, documents to transport the merchandise to the port of export must be filed and approved by CBP. Standard export documents must then be filed at the time the merchandise is actually exported.

Source: *U.S. Customs and Border Protection: Importing into the United States: A Guide for Commercial Importers,* November, 2006, various pages.

CBP Forms Required for FTZ and Non-FTZ Users
(Text Box A-2)

For all FTZ and Non-FTZ Users:

- **Form 3461**, for every formal customs entry into the United States, lets Customs know what products importers might enter during the week. Each form is accompanied by a merchandise processing fee equal to %0.3464 of the value of the imports, not to exceed $485. In FTZs, an estimated 3461 must also be filed prior to the start of the week if the zone is filing weekly entries.

- **Form 7501**—the official entry form declaring tariffs owed (together with payment) within 10 days.

Additional for FTZ Users:

- **Form 214** for admission of goods into an FTZ.

- **Form 7512** (automated in-bond form) for the in-bond transfer of goods to, from, or between zones or for manipulation or storage, or out of the country for export. (Bond guarantees that money has been set aside to pay tariffs owed, reflects the value and the volume of the cargo, and "insures" the dutiable value of the goods)

Source: CBP, Foreign-Trade Zones Manual, p. 203, and discussions with the U.S. FTZ Board and the Census.

Table A-2. Key Data on U.S. FTZs, 1993, 1997, and 2010-2012

	1993	1997	2010	2011	2012
Employees in Zones	292,000	310,000	320,000	340,000	370,000
Active FTZ Projects	122	141	168	171	174
Firms Using a Zone	2,700	3,550	2,400	2,800	3,200
Total domestic and foreign Merchandise Received (Current $ Bil.)	$104	$178	$534	$641	$732

Source: U.S. FTZ Board, Annual Reports.

Note: Between 1997 and 2012, the overall increase in zone use, along with the particular expansion by the oil sector, has resulted in a decrease in the number of firms using zones, (from 3,550 to 3,200). However, it has also resulted in an increase in employment, (from 310,000 to 370,000) and a four-fold increase in the current dollar value of merchandise received/shipped.

Author Contact Information

Mary Jane Bolle
Specialist in International Trade and Finance
mjbolle@crs.loc.gov, 7-7753

Brock R. Williams
Analyst in International Trade and Finance
bwilliams@crs.loc.gov, 7-1157

Acknowledgments

William H. Cooper, James K. Jackson, Mary A, Irace, and Vivian C. Jones participated in review of this report; Amber H. Wilhelm, Sandra L. Edwards, and Mallary A. Stouffer provided graphics, stylistic, and editorial assistance.

.